Searchlight
BOOKS™

What
Are Energy
Sources?

Finding Out about

Hydropower

Matt Doeden

Lerner Publications Company
Minneapolis

Lerner Publications Company
A division of Lerner Publishing Group, Inc.
241 First Avenue North
Minneapolis, MN 55401 USA

For reading levels and more information, look up this title at www.lernerbooks.com.

Library of Congress Cataloging-in-Publication Data

Doeden, Matt, author.
    Finding out about hydropower / by Matt Doeden.
       pages   cm. — (Searchlight books™ — What are energy sources?)
    Includes index.
    ISBN 978–1–4677–3659–6 (lib. bdg. : alk. paper)
    ISBN 978–1–4677–4639–7 (eBook)
    1. Water-power—Juvenile literature. I. Title.
  TC147.D64 2015
  333.91'4—dc23   2013037868

Manufactured in the United States of America
1 — BP — 7/15/14

Contents

Chapter 1

WHAT IS HYDROPOWER?

Imagine wading into the current of a fast-moving river. The water rushes around you. It pushes on your feet and your legs. If the current is strong enough, it can knock you over. Then it can carry you down the river.

Wading into a river with a strong current is hard work. What can happen if the current is too strong?

The force of the water against your legs comes from kinetic energy. All moving objects have this energy. We can use the kinetic energy of moving water to produce electricity. This is called hydropower.

When you run, you have kinetic energy.

Where Does the Energy Come From?

Energy doesn't come from just anywhere. So how does a rushing river get its kinetic energy? It comes from the sun! But it is not direct. There are a few steps along the way.

Hydropower comes from the water cycle, which is powered by the sun.

Water from the ocean evaporates and creates clouds.

Heat from the sun's rays powers the water cycle. That's how water moves around the world. Think of the sun beating down on an ocean or a lake. The sun's heat causes some of the water to turn into vapor. The vapor collects and forms clouds.

Many of these clouds move over land. Some of the vapor falls as rain or snow. Rain and melted snow run off into rivers. The rivers empty into oceans and lakes. Then the cycle starts all over again. As long as the sun keeps shining, Earth's water will keep moving.

Rain is another phase of the water cycle.

Where Is Hydropower Produced?

Any source of moving water can produce hydropower. Even small streams can create it. But large, fast-moving rivers create the most.

A RIVER WITH RAPIDLY FLOWING WATER CAN CREATE A LOT OF HYDROPOWER.

An object's kinetic energy depends on its size and its speed. A speeding car has a lot more of it than a speeding bicycle. The same is true for water. The more water a river has, the more energy we can get from it. That's why most hydropower plants, or hydro plants, are on big rivers.

You have kinetic energy when you ride your bike.

Chapter 2

PRODUCING HYDROPOWER

People have been using the energy in moving water for thousands of years. People built waterwheels on rushing rivers in ancient Rome and China.

The ancient Egyptians used waterwheels to collect energy. How long have people been using energy from moving water?

The waterwheels had spinning blades or buckets. The moving water pushed on them and spun the wheel. A stone was attached to the wheel to crush grain. A blade could be attached to cut wood as the wheel spun.

Waterwheels helped people crush grain more easily.

Few people use waterwheels in modern times. Instead, we use dams and other machines to turn the water's energy into electricity.

This large dam can generate a lot of electricity.

Hydro Plants

In the late 1800s, people learned they could turn a river's kinetic energy into electricity. They built the first hydro plants. The electricity the plants created powered nearby homes and buildings.

This is an abandoned hydro plant in Oregon.

Today, hydro plants use three main parts. They are the dam, the reservoir, and the generator. It all starts with the dam. Large dams stretch across a river. They block the flow of the river's water.

The Hoover Dam stretches across the Colorado River on the Arizona-Nevada border.

The reservoir forms as water backs up behind the dam. The reservoir is a way of storing the water and its energy. That way, hydro plants always have a supply of water to use as they need energy.

Boats float along a reservoir created by a dam.

Channels are built inside the dam. The channels angle downward. They can be opened or closed to control the flow of water through the dam. Water travels through the channels and passes over machines called turbines.

Hydroelectric turbines are very large.

Turbines have large blades. The moving water spins the blades. Each turbine is connected to a generator. This machine turns the energy into electricity. The faster the water is moving, the more electricity the generator makes.

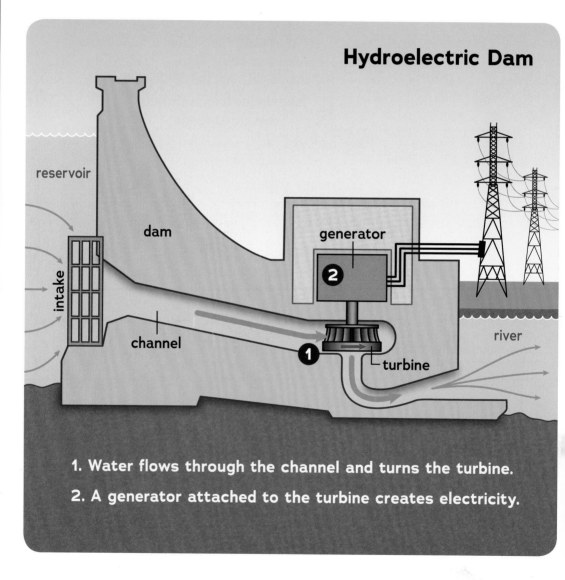

Hydroelectric Dam

reservoir

dam

intake

channel

generator

2

1

turbine

river

1. Water flows through the channel and turns the turbine.
2. A generator attached to the turbine creates electricity.

ROR Plants

Creating reservoirs can be harmful to the environment. They change the flow of a river. They can disrupt wildlife that live in and near the river. Run-of-the-river (ROR) plants work without creating reservoirs. ROR plants are often built near waterfalls of fast-moving rivers.

ROR PLANTS ALLOW RIVERS TO FLOW NATURALLY. THAT'S GOOD FOR WILDLIFE.

ROR plants move some water away from rivers. This water turns turbines. The water is then returned to the rivers downstream. The amount of power produced depends on the flow of the rivers. When the rivers are low, little or no power may be produced. ROR plants are better for the environment. But they are not as reliable as regular hydro plants.

ROR plants don't have reservoirs like regular hydro plants.

Chapter 3

THE PROS AND CONS OF HYDROPOWER

Hydropower has been around for a long time. It is cheap and reliable. It is renewable, so we won't run out of it. Like all energy sources, it has pros and cons.

Hydropower has many benefits. Can you name two?

The Environment

In many ways, hydropower is good for the environment. It creates electricity without burning fossil fuels such as coal, natural gas, and oil. Burning these fuels creates pollution. It also puts carbon dioxide into the air.

The burning of coal causes air pollution.

Most scientists agree that the release of this gas is causing Earth's climate to warm. Too much warming could be a disaster. We could get more heat waves, droughts, and wildfires. Sea level would rise too. Hydro plants don't release carbon dioxide. So they don't contribute to a warming Earth.

Droughts can dry out crops.

But building dams changes rivers and the land around them. Reservoirs spread out over what was once dry land. That kills trees and other plants. It wipes out the homes of animals and sometimes people.

Reservoirs change the landscape around a dam. Water covers areas that were once dry land.

This riverbank has eroded due to a lack of sediment in the river.

Dams can also affect a river downstream. Healthy rivers carry sediment. Sediment is a mixture of rocks, sand, and dirt. Dams block sediment from continuing down a river. When a river stops carrying sediment downstream, its banks can erode. This can be harmful to wildlife that depend on the river.

Trouble for Salmon

Fish and other animals that travel up and down rivers also suffer. One such fish is salmon. Salmon live most of their lives in the ocean. But they swim up rivers to lay their eggs in spots called spawning grounds.

These salmon are swimming upstream to lay their eggs.

Sometimes dams get in the salmon's way. The fish can't reach their spawning grounds to lay eggs. Many die just trying to find a way over the dams.

Salmon can easily get caught up in a dam and die trying to get to spawning grounds.

And it's not safe going downstream either. Many young salmon die when they swim into spinning turbines. Scientists have found big drops in salmon populations in many dammed rivers. That's bad for people and animals that need the salmon for food.

A DAM MAKES SWIMMING DOWNSTREAM DANGEROUS FOR YOUNG SALMON.

People have tried to solve this problem by building fish ladders on dams. These passages allow fish to swim around dams by jumping up small steps. Fish ladders have helped preserve fish populations in some rivers. But it's not a perfect solution. The dams still pose a threat to young salmon returning to the ocean. And not all the fish make it up the ladders.

Fish can swim up this fish ladder at Rocky Reach Dam in Washington.

Dam Failure

Another danger from hydro plants comes from dam failure. When a dam breaks, all the water in its reservoir rushes down the river. This can cause huge floods.

Reservoirs hold huge amounts of water. That makes flooding a serious danger if a dam collapses.

The worst dam failure in US history happened in Pennsylvania in 1889. The South Fork Dam collapsed. About 20 million tons (18 million metric tons) of water rushed downstream. That's more water than seven thousand Olympic-sized swimming pools can hold. The water flooded the nearby town of Johnstown. More than two thousand people died.

This illustration shows a town damaged by floodwaters after the South Fork Dam collapsed.

Other failures have happened since. But dam technology has improved a lot recently. A major dam hasn't failed in the United States since the 1970s. Still, failure remains a danger to anyone living downstream of a hydro plant.

A dam collapse upstream would likely wipe out the homes alongside this river.

Availability

In some places, large rivers are common. Hydropower can be easily produced in these places. But other places aren't near large rivers. So not a lot of hydropower can be created. People living in these places have to find other sources of energy.

Dry deserts are far from rivers. Hydropower isn't available, so residents need other energy sources.

Chapter 4

HYDROPOWER IN THE FUTURE

About 7 percent of US electricity comes from hydropower. It is the largest renewable energy source. And hydropower could be used even more. The United States has about eighty thousand dams. Less than 3 percent produce power. Turning them into hydro plants would provide more clean energy.

This is an irrigation dam. Why might it be good to turn this dam into a hydro plant?

Alternative Energy

Many experts say that alternative energy sources are the key to the world's future energy needs. Fossil fuels make up most of the world's energy supply. But these are nonrenewable. And over time, fossil fuels will become rarer and more expensive to collect.

Burning coal at a power plant releases carbon dioxide into the air.

We need to find other sources of energy. Since hydropower is renewable, it could be a big piece of the puzzle. But hydropower can't do it alone. It's available only in some areas. And we can build only so many hydro plants.

HYDROPOWER IS JUST ONE OF SEVERAL CLEAN ENERGY SOURCES AVAILABLE TODAY.

Other alternative energy sources will have to work alongside hydropower. These include solar, wind, and nuclear power. Many people dream of a day when these alternative energy sources replace fossil fuels altogether.

Workers install solar panels.

Glossary

alternative energy source: a source of energy other than traditional fossil fuels

erode: to wear away

fossil fuel: a fuel such as coal, natural gas, or oil that was formed over millions of years from the remains of dead plants and animals

generator: a machine that turns mechanical energy into electricity

kinetic energy: the energy associated with a moving object

nonrenewable: not able to be replenished. Once a nonrenewable form of energy is gone, it is used up for good.

reliable: offering consistently good performance

renewable: able to be replenished over time

reservoir: a body of water that builds up behind a dam

sediment: the rock, sand, and dirt that are carried by a river

spawning ground: a place where salmon swim to lay their eggs

turbine: a machine with blades that converts the energy from a moving gas or fluid, such as water, into mechanical energy

vapor: a substance that is normally a liquid or a solid that is suspended in the air, such as steam

water cycle: the movement of water around the world

Learn More about Hydropower

Books

Bailey, Gerry. *Out of Energy*. New York: Gareth Stevens, 2011. Learn more about alternatives to fossil fuels, from geothermal to solar, and find out how you can use energy more efficiently.

Doeden, Matt. *Finding Out about Coal, Oil, and Natural Gas*. Minneapolis: Lerner Publications, 2015. Fossil fuels remain our main source of energy. Learn more about how they form, how they're collected, and the pros and cons of using them.

Fridell, Ron. *Earth-Friendly Energy*. Minneapolis: Lerner Publications, 2009. Explore alternative energy sources, such as hydropower, wind, and solar, and discover how these energy sources may power our future.

Websites

Energy Kids—Hydropower
http://www.eia.gov/kids/energy.cfm?page=hydropower_home-basics
The US Energy Information Administration's page on hydropower includes diagrams and maps that will teach you more about hydropower.

How Hydropower Plants Work
http://science.howstuffworks.com/environmental/energy/hydropower-plant.htm
Check out a detailed description of how hydropower plants work.

A Student's Guide to Global Climate Change—Water Energy
http://www.epa.gov/climatestudents/solutions/technologies/water.html
At this US Environmental Protection Agency site, read more about the different ways electricity can be produced from water energy.

Index

Photo Acknowledgments

The images in this book are used with the permission of: © iStock/Thinkstock, p. 4, 21;
© iStockphoto.com/Blacqbook, p. 5; © iStockphoto.com/Logray-2008, p. 6; © iStockphoto.com/
TommL, p. 7; © iStockphoto.com/bethsp, p. 8; © iStockphoto.com/tupungato, p. 9; © Dimitry
Naumov/Shutterstock.com, p. 10; © Sheila Terry/Science Source, p. 11; © Interfoto/Alamy, p. 12;
© iStockphoto.com/namibelephant, p. 13; © Jit Lim/Alamy, p. 14; © iStockphoto.com/ksteen5,
p. 15; US Army Corps of Engineers, Norfolk District, p. 16, 20; © iStockphoto.com/photosbyjim,
p. 17; © Laura Westlund/Independent Picture Service, p. 18; © Johan Swanepoel/Shutterstock.com,
p. 19; © abutyrin/Shutterstock.com, p. 22; © MaxyM/Shutterstock.com, p. 23; Inna Felker/iStock/
Thinkstock, p. 24; © Iain Frazer/Shutterstock.com, p. 25; © Sekar B/Shutterstock.com, p. 26;
© iStockphoto.com/Baxternator, p. 27; © iStockphoto.com/ssucsy, p. 28; © iStockphoto.com/
ajphoto, p. 29; © iStockphoto.com/photoquest7, p. 30; Francis Schell and Thomas Hogan/Wikimedia
Commons, p. 31; © iStockphoto.com/AustinMirage, p. 32; © iStockphoto.com/Tim Abbott, p. 33;
© iStockphoto.com/ineb1599, p. 34; © Doin Oakenhelm/Shutterstock.com, p. 35; © iStockphoto.
com/miljko, p. 36.

Front Cover: © Bigsky06/Dreamstime.com

Main body text set in Adrianna Regular 14/20
Typeface provided by Chank